Seasons

Noelle Dawn Cosby

BookLeaf
Publishing

India | USA | UK

Presentation by *BookLeaf Publishing*

Web: www.bookleafpub.com

E-mail: info@bookleafpub.com

ISBN: 9789357448086

First edition 2021

This book is dedicated to my husband and best
friend Jason. If it were not for his patient love,
care, and encouragement, I may still be lonely
and afraid. For that, Jason, you are my hero!

ACKNOWLEDGEMENT

I want to thank my Creator King, Jesus, for loving me just the way I am and helping me to grow in love everyday. My children Kara, Gavin, Guinevere, and Obed for their continual love, support, and prayer. My spiritual father, pastor, and friend Mark C. for believing in me enough to give me the courage to share my art with the world. My other "mom" Destani C. for showing me what a life lived in freedom in Christ looks like. Also, last but not least, my parents Georgia Ann and Victor Hamelin for doing their very best to support my creative endeavors their entire life.

Mother

They call me mother
They call me earth
They call me nature
The give me worth
They look upon my mountains
They explore my deepest seas
They gaze upon my wonders
They wonder how I came to be
I call You Beauty
I call You Creator
I call upon Your very name
Even the rocks that I am made of sing aloud a
song of praise
I do not wonder where I came from
I do not wonder how I was made
Your love formed all my seasides, anchored the
sands to my shorelines
You cover me in fragrant flora creating safety
for the fauna, life dancing on my fault lines and
bringing forth the rains
Oh how I long for them to know You, to know
Your love, to see Your face
Whose Spirit fashioned all my caverns, who
causes the sun itself to wake
Oh that they would tell Your stories, oh that they
would know Your name

This is my prayer, beloved Maker, for this I cry out till the end of days

Fireside

Do you see her dancing, she's dancing in the
wind
Wild, whimsy, whisping, waves inviting warmth
within
Waiting for a faithful friend to cozy by her side
In hopes they would encourage her to burn
strong throughout the night
Surrounded by blissful voices singing songs of
victory
She hosts stories of the days gone by, as she
shifts with every breeze
Her vibrant colors, fierce and frail, provide
peace in our darkest hour
Filling up the atmosphere, her fragrance wild
with power
Oh, how she longs to stay a flame, how she
craves a breath to keep her
Aware without your tender care she will wither
and bewilder
Burn on my love, burn bright, burn warm, burn
free and everlasting
The fireside is calling you, for it is you whom
she is longing

Tundra

Shadows in the valley are difficult to bear
They follow me in hollows and around the
corners stare
Dark grayish willow figures on crystal mountain
sides
Whispering their sadness as the wistful winds
draws nigh
The days are bitter, cold, forlorn
The nights no better yet
Winter herself is struck with fear as grief
becomes beset
What shall we do, what shall we say when life's
Tundra comes acalling
I say, "fear not, for the time is short and the
Spring is soon and coming"

Snowflake

Every facet fashioned for flowing with the wind
Not one like another, all unique and none
chagrin
Wild winter colors crystallize within
Creativity meets whimsy, the frenzy now begins
Each uniquely crafted an elegant design
Swirling in a storm cloud refracting the Divine
Every one exhaling a song from the inside
Some a wild roar, others a lullaby
Different and beautiful
Peculiar, alive, and free
Dancing through the atmosphere
Releasing joy and peace

Fancy

All that glitters, all that's gold, shiny fancy
things
Hiding who we really are with smiles and
diamond rings
Fancy people in fancy clothes, painted hair and
faces
Taught to conceal who we really are for fear of
social disgraces
"Your mask, it fits so well my dear, it
compliments your eyes. Just make sure it glitters
more than other passers by. You'll need the
newest labeled wares to become the perfect fit.
Trust me, love, take my advice or you will be ill
equipped."
Perfect people with perfect lives are vice of
many fools
And many people everywhere are drawn to gems
and jewels
If I were you, I would become wise of their wily
ways
Simply stay true to who your are and how it was
that you were made

Winter

The time has come, the winds blow in
The moments pass with haste
There is nothing left but nakedness awaiting a
cold embrace
The earth becomes so sleepy, she lays her head
to rest
Beneath pillowy white blankets she finds peace
in what feels like death
Allowing herself to cave to the frigid ice cold
breeze
She chooses not to fight the change, but to
welcome it with ease
For this is not the first time she has weathered
through the storm
She has learnt that winter's wonders are found in
winter's darkest morns

Flourish

To flourish is to be as a water lily
Roots stretching deep beneath
I connect with the Divine as I rest upon the
shimmering waves
My petals absorbing radiant light as I behold
Him
I find no other source of life as I float above the
water
Releasing an intoxicating fragrance drawing on
His love
I am nourished by the gentleness of the One who
fashioned me
I hear my lover sing over me, I dance for Him
I begin to radiate His uncompromisable nature,
reflecting His glory
I flourish

Prism

Colors of wonder, beautifully bright
Whimsical, wild, a wondrous delight
Stretching her arms from far too wide
She welcomes the rain as the sun shines
Where has she come from
Where has she gone
Fascination awaits her unknown return
Oh to behold her
Oh to befriend
Where does she begin
Where will she end
This glorious ray of infinite light
She welcomes the day
She despises the night
She colors the wind
And paints the sky
So beautiful, so wild, the rainbow and I

Bloom

Unfolding delicate petals
Unwrapped, peeled back
Fragrance released
Sweet, floral, spice
Receiving light
Soft, lovely, beautiful
Disbursing desire
Adorned, shimmering, awestruck
She sees
A new world, a new life

Altar

Your mind on the altar
Your ear to His chest
His heart beats with wonder
You enter His rest
Succumbing to mercy
New everyday
Knowing that joy
Is a heartbeat away
Wholeness in grace-life
Cancels your fear
With your mind on the altar
He can come near
Not mind over matter
Or wherewithal poise
Only resting in Him
Will quiet the noise
Put your mind on the altar
Give your thoughts a day free
Rejoice in His goodness
Celebrate peace

Spring

Bursting with beauty between sunshine and rain
With soft tender mercies, earth arises again
Welcoming song birds to nest in the trees
Delighting in new life, coming forth from
beneath
Reminding the moon to shine brighter each eve
Revealing new stars we've yet to see
Delicate fragrances sweep through the air
As morning glories unfold their petals in prayer
All creation cries loud, a voice to be heard
"We're alive! We're awake, it's now time for new
birth"

Deeper

One voice, many waters
One sound, one frequency
I come alive when I hear it
The earthquakes inside me
Passion stirring fire burning
I surrender to the waves
Carried into deeper waters
I catch my breath and cling to faith
I share a breath with my creator
We release the sound within
Crying out with untamed passion
Caution thrown into the wind
I feel peace like no other
Peace eliminating fear
I hear a call to come in deeper
Into dimensions I disappear

Willow

Rooted deep in waters shallow
Filled with strength, gentility
Your whimsical movements welcome the weary
They find rest in your shadows and company
Your silence causes hearts to still
As you sway softly in the breeze
Even when the storms set in
Nothing steals your steady peace
Absorbing all the river gives you
Taking in all you need
Never shy to receive your portion
You are happy just to be a tree

Collage

Life, not picture perfect.
Yet, so many times and in so many ways we are
led to believe that everything is always fine.
Posting pictures of our finest hours and making
believe this is our everyday.
Is this really OK?
Life is meant to be a collage of greatest days,
and moments of dismay.
Celebrations and sorrows, where there is always
a chance of tomorrows being better than todays.
So how do we change?
I say, take time to pray. Seek out why you were
made.
Let your authentic self out to play with no fear
of what "they" might say.
Maybe in some way you could become more
than an overcomer by simply living your life in
complete truth, just today.

Shine

Radiant glowing amber waves
Rising at the dawn
Earth warming with her smile
Shadows run at her return
Lighting the horizon
Awakening the sea
Giving life to all creation
Night-time darkness in retreat
Oh the sunrise glory beams
Her beauty unexplained
Crimson orange-hued glistening bliss
Light-kissed brilliant face
None can escape her wondrous fiery gaze
For daybreak has begun as the depths of
darkness fade
Shine on, shine forth, shine bright my love
Forever shines the Sun
She warms the earth and atmosphere inviting life
to come

Summer

Fireflies, flowers, mid-summer delights
Star gazing by riversides, sun-shines into the
night
Dancing in shadows, running through rain
Unhindered freedom, life seems without pain
The earth moving slowly, hearts full of romance
Looking deep in another, then begin holding
hands
Sharing their secrets, whispering dreams
Souls entwine, hearts flutter and gleam
The magic of summer fills us with love
Oh, let's take with us when Autumn does come

Gather

Hello old friend, how have you been, it has been
quite some time
Come on in, sit down, and then share your heart
with mine
Oh how I have missed our long talks over coffee
by the fire
Let us take our time today to reminisce and
conspire
About the summer and the rain, the truth-tellers
and the liars
Let's talk till dawn, we'll share our dreams as
we sit here round the fire
Life goes by, we miss the mark of sharing time
together
How will we take time to slow and begin again
to gather
Grab your friends, draw them near for time goes
by so fast
We only have but moments, let's try to make
them last

Fade

As the brisk cool air blows, Summer's grip sets me free
Fading from bright emerald green to dark yet so lovely
Letting go of all I know, carried by the winds
Falling, floating through the air, where will this journey end?
My auburn shade and brittle frame land softly on the ground
I begin to wither, yet I feel quite safe and sound
Back to the place from which I grew steady from a seed
The earth again welcomes me to fulfill my purposed deed

Harvest

Amber hues dancing, the harvest begins
White wild with fury, the grains have come in
Hearkening glory, beckoning peace
Welcoming us to take part in the feast
Setting the table for family and friend
We celebrate goodness as mercy steps in
Remembering all that it's cost to receive
Our portion is given because we've believed
Overflowing our storehouse, abundant in seed
We now give to others with thanks to the King

Wind

Can you hear him whisper, gentle as a dove
Swirling in the atmosphere churning up above
Touch just like a feather, soft and subtle on my
skin
I am not certain where he is headed, or even
where he has been
It is true that when he's needed, he shows up on
the scene
Moving things to where they'll rest from where
they had once been
Even when he is moving swift, I am quite at ease
For the center of his presence brings a restful
kind of peace
I am sure that you may wonder who my friend
could be
He is the winsome, whirling wind and when
with him I am free

Autumn

The warm night turns into a cold brisk eve
The sun sets sooner than the farmers need
The wind begins stirring, and as the leaves start
to change
Deep reds and burnt oranges paint the ground
again
Campfires are burning and friendships renew
Yes, let the winds blow, let the warm drinks
brew
For summer is gone and we bid her "Adieu"
Autumn, my friend, we welcome you